More Memories

of

Wakefield

Part of the

Memories

series

The Publishers would like to thank the following companies for supporting
the production of this book

Craven Fawcett (1997) Limited

Job Earnshaw & Bros Ltd

Dunlop Slazenger International Limited

National Coal Mining Museum

Normanton Brick Company Limited

Pinderfields & Pontefract Hospitals NHS Trust

Wilsons of Wakefield

Warburtons

Woodhead Investments & Development Services Limited

First published in Great Britain by True North Books Limited
Units 3 - 5 Heathfield Industrial Park
Elland West Yorkshire
HX5 9AE
Tel. 01422 377977
© Copyright: True North Books Limited 1999

ISBN 1 900463 89 X

Text, design and origination by True North Books Limited
Printed and bound by The Amadeus Press Limited

Memories are made of this

emories. We all have them: people, places and events, some good and some bad. Our memories of the place where we grew up are usually tucked away in a very special place in our mind. The best are probably connected with our childhood and youth, when we longed to be grown up and paid no attention to adults who told us to enjoy being young, as these were the best years of our lives. We look back now and realise that they were right.

Old photographs bring our memories flooding back - coronations and celebrations; talking pictures, Technicolor and television; the war years, rationing, and the shared hopes and fears which created such a warm community spirit; buying things made of nylon and plastic; fashions which took trouser-bottoms and hemlines from drainpipes and mini-skirts to the other extreme; Doris Day, Acker Bilk, Elvis Presley and the Beatles; the jitterbug, the tango and discos; Ford Populars and Minis; decimalisation. Life changed so much over the years. Some changes were big, some small; some altered our lives in ways we never anticipated. Who in the early days of motoring could have foreseen the motorways and traffic systems of the latter decades of the 20th century? Did any of us realise, when we first saw a computer, what a tremendous impact they would have on our lives? Self-service supermarkets and frozen food made our lives easier - but at the expense of our friendly little corner shops. Nostalgia is always such a mixture of feelings . . . We hope that the collection of pictures in this book will remind you of happy days in bygone eras - and who knows, you might even have been there when one of the photographs was taken!

Contents

Wakefield through the years

Nothing ever stays the same, and as conditions change many towns and cities around the country lost direction and dwindled in importance. Wakefield proved to be the exception, and over the years developed a remarkable ability to adapt to change. For around 700 years the town was the capital of the Yorkshire woollen industry, yet with the Industrial Revolution much of the wool trade moved towards Bradford and Leeds. By the 19th century, development of the canal had led to Wakefield's growth as an agricultural centre, possessing the largest corn market in the north of England. By the turn of the 20th century, however, the trade had declined and the corn market building was given over to other uses. Coal has been mined around Wakefield since around the 14th century - and as we all know, the industry has had its own particular challenges to face. Through it all, Wakefield came to terms with the situation, adapted, changed direction, and proved its staying power.

Wakefield has had a picturesque past. More than 600 years ago wake-plays - thought to have given the town its name - were performed, acting out the joys, sorrows and beliefs of its people. The beautiful church of All Saints was built - and twice almost lost to us in the reforming zeal of the 16th century and again during the Civil War. The year 1888 was destined, however, to be a year of triumph; All Saints church became Wakefield Cathedral, and Wakefield town became the city of Wakefield.

This collection of fascinating images deals with the last half of the 20th century, and has been put together to take our readers on a trip down Memory Lane. We are fortunate that the 20th century was so well chronicled: the day the champagne corks popped when Wakefield Trinity won the Rugby League Challenge Cup in 1946; the collapse of the 16th century Six Chimneys in 1941; the opening of Wakefield's first supermarket; the buses and trains we rode on - all find their way into the pages of this book.

We hope that you will read and enjoy 'More Memories of Wakefield' - and remember that history is still in the making.

Around the city centre

The Bull Ring has in its long life gone through more metamorphoses than your average cabbage white butterfly! From the buildings beyond Queen Victoria's statue to the fine old vehicles in this 1940s view, younger readers will find the scene quite unfamiliar. Plenty of refreshment was on offer around the Bull Ring at the time. Briggs' Cafe and the Regent Cafe vied for trade in a block of old properties which was demolished after World War II, while if you wanted something a little stronger than tea and coffee the Griffin Hotel competed with the Strafford Arms, on the left of the photograph. A sharp eye will spot Fred Zeigler's pork butcher's shop in the background. A major piece of national history is connected with Mr Zeigler, who was one of the original major shareholders in the company which was destined in 1965 to become Asda superstores. While many of us will focus our attention on the shops, others will be more interested in the cars of yesteryear pictured here. The Austin Cambridge on the right was a popular car, widely used at the time by taxi drivers. It was later to evolve and emerge in a new boxy style which was virtually indistinguishable from the Morris Oxford.

Above: A different frontage than today's graces the Strafford Arms Hotel and the other shops on the corner of Northgate as we look at the Bull Ring from the Cathedral Tower. There is no statue of Queen Victoria in the Ring; she has been moved to Clarence Park, not to return until 1985. The later restructuring of the area will involve the buildings to the left being removed and replaced by more modern structures. The bus stop on Northgate is from Leeds and the return journey, as we can see from the bus circling the roundabout involved almost a tour of the city taking in the Cathedral before it set off for Leeds. The background to Northgate is more developed now though it appears to be today mostly car parks. The area to the left towards Wood Street, containing the old West Riding county and Wakefield borough buildings and the police station, is the administrative heart of the town and has kept its shape and its importance. It will be 1985 before this traffic maze of the Bull Ring is cut through and a pedestrian scheme slices it in half, making Lower Northgate no longer a through road. Some time to go before this occurs.

Right: The Cathedral - Wakefield's pride - dominates the skyline in this rooftop view captured on 10th May 1932. It was 1888 when the church of All Saints became Wakefield Cathedral, and parts of the building date back to the 14th century. Protestant zeal during the Reformation was responsible for the destruction of many of the church's beautiful paintings and statues - and thereby hangs an interesting tale. Two hundred years later, in 1756, a householder in Northgate discovered twenty-five figures - presumably from the church - hidden away in the loft of his house. Some brave person back in Tudor times had risked his or her life to preserve the artefacts that symbolised the old religion. Sadly, the figures were destroyed. From the interesting gables of the insurance offices in the bottom left corner, Cross Street leads away past the Prince Albert wing of the old Clayton Hospital. The hospital owes its name and its existence to Thomas Clayton, a successful 18th century Wakefield businessman, whose dispensary in Northgate eventually became a sizeable hospital which quickly grew and expanded. A brand new 60-bed hospital was opened in 1879.

Two of Wakefield's finest buildings, the Town Hall and the County Hall, dominate the skyline of this pigeon's-eye view of the Bull Ring and Northgate in former years. Cars were parked along both sides of the road when the scene was recorded, and apart from public transport little traffic was on the move in Northgate. How things change!

The civic centre has long been the city's pride, though Victorian Wakefield had a very long wait before the promised Town Hall actually materialised. Part of the site for the new building was

Events of the 1930s

HOT OFF THE PRESS

The years of the 1930s saw Adolf Hitler's sickening anti-Jewish campaign echoed in the streets of Britain. On 19th October 1936 Oswald Mosley's 7,000-strong British Union of Fascists clashed head on with thousands of Jews and Communists in London, resulting in 80 people being injured in the ensuing battle. Mosley and his 'blackshirts' later rampaged through the streets beating up Jews and smashing the windows of their businesses.

GETTING AROUND

At the beginning of the decade many believed that the airship was the transport of the future. The R101 airship, however, loaded with thousands of cubic metres of hydrogen, crashed in France on its maiden flight in 1930. Forty-eight passengers and crew lost their lives. In 1937 the Hindenburg burst into flames - the entire disaster caught on camera and described by a distraught reporter. The days of the airship were numbered.

SPORTING CHANCE

In 1939 British racing driver Sir Malcolm Campbell hit the headlines when he captured the world's water-speed record for the third time in 'Bluebird' - all his cars were given the same name. A racing driver who set world speed records both on land and on water, Sir Malcolm established world land-speed records no fewer than nine times. His son Donald went on to set further records, tragically dying in 1967 when his speedboat - also named 'Bluebird' - crashed.

purchased more than 20 years before the foundation stone was laid. In 1877, a nation-wide competition was held to choose a design; London architect T E Collcutt was declared the winner, and the stately new Town Hall was opened three years later, in October 1880. Before long, work began on the elegant County Hall, which was declared open in 1898.

Events of the 1930s

SCIENCE AND DISCOVERY
By observing the heavens, astronomers had long believed that there in the constellation of Gemini lay a new planet, so far undis-covered. They began to search for the elusive planet, and a special astro-nomical camera was built for the purpose. The planet Pluto was discovered by amateur astronomer Clyde Tombaugh in 1930, less than a year later.

WHAT'S ON?
In this heyday of the cinema, horrified audiences were left gasping at the sight of Fay Wray in the clutches of the giant ape in the film 'King Kong', released in 1933. Very different but just as gripping was the gutsy 1939 American Civil War romance 'Gone with the Wind'. Gable's parting words, 'Frankly, my dear, I don't give a damn' went down in history.

ROYAL WATCH
The talking point of the early 1930s was the affair of the Prince of Wales, who later became King Edward VIII, and American divorcee Wallis Simpson. Faced with a choice, Edward gave up his throne for 'the woman I love' and spent the remainder of his life in exile. Many supported him, though they might not have been as keen to do so if they had been aware of his Nazi sympathies, kept strictly under wraps at the time.

Queen Victoria's back is turned towards the queue of passengers (and a bus conductor) waiting hopefully for the Number 10 bus to Sandal. In the meantime, however, they appear to have found something of interest to gain their attention. We can't spot anything unusual enough to attract every eye; we can say with a degree of certainty that it would not have been the outline of the

long-departed monarch - the people of Wakefield were so used to seeing her statue in the Bull Ring that they hardly noticed the old Queen any more. There is a saying, however, that we don't miss a thing until it's gone, and this applied to the statue of Queen Victoria. When it was carried away to Thornes Park there were many unhappy rumblings, and when the Bull Ring was eventually redeveloped in the 1980s, West Yorkshire County Council suggested installing a modern sculpture. Wakefield councillors, however, wanted the old Queen back - and happily they got their way.

Bottom: The story of the growth and prosperity of towns and cities is more often than not reflected in its buildings. Wakefield, as it began to flourish in the eighteenth and nineteenth centuries, built in its main streets banks, shops, meeting halls, inns, warehouses, markets and places of entertainment to accommodate the new age. Railways came and brought travellers to the town so hotels were established close by to accommodate them. Westgate was a typical example of a thriving street and we can still see evidence of that today. There is at the corner of Smyth Street Unity House, Wakefield's first Co-op, established by prison officers. The Grand Theatre is opposite, designed by Frank Matcham, responsible for, amongst others, the long-gone Grand Theatre in Keighley. There was at the corner of Queen Street this building, the Corn Exchange, serving in this 1961 photograph, a multitude of purposes. A building society, a cinema, roller skating, wrestling, shops and bar were some of the activities for which it was used. In some ways it was in its latter days an asset to Wakefield in that it did serve many purposes, though they do appear to have been short-term.

Right: This upper part of Westgate is now a conservation area. There were so many fine buildings in the street that there was a need to ensure they remained, architecturally at least, as close to the original intent of their builders. This grand building, the original Corn Exchange, still retains vestiges of its former grandeur. It has served many purposes throughout the years. Wrestling, roller skating, once the Grand Electric Cinema, known

affectionately as the 'Ranch', too much Gary Cooper and John Wayne perhaps, and compare those activities to the scene in 1849 of the great Free Trade dinner held there. On this wet January day in 1962 the traffic problems which would beset Wakefield and all other towns and cities are not yet evident. Crossing the road, parking your car and unloading your van are not hazardous occupations. Certainly there are one or two interesting cars here. The Austin Cambridge, Morris Oxford and the MG all had virtually the same kind of body, the MG would obviously possess the more sporty look. The Ford car, predecessor of the Escort, had two models had that time - the Popular with two doors and the superior sounding Prefect with four. An interesting photograph in many ways with perhaps the old Corn Exchange serving as reminder of what this part of Wakefield was like nearly 40 years ago.

all city and town treasures should possess. This 1958 photograph gives another chance to look at the road from Leeds into the city. There is the new bus station but no car parks, either ground level or multi storey. The Bull Ring, somewhere below our keen young photographer, has yet to change. It did have the Intercon Night club. Later that name was changed to the Moonraker. During the week Wakefield's teenyboppers went to the Mecca later known as Tiffany's or, if you really wanted to appear 'cool', you arranged to meet her inside 'Tiffs'.

Top: Towards the end of the long summer holidays was traditionally the time when the mothers of Wakefield badgered, bullied or bribed their children into a visit to Kingswells, where they were kitted out in the uniforms of Wakefield Girls' High School and other upper schools in the area. Readers well remember that sinking 'back to school' feeling, which during August was tinged with the excitement of starting afresh in a different year, or even a different school. Southcotts was Wakefield's other supplier of school uniforms, and when spring arrived, and with it the buying of girls' summer uniform, everyone knew which shop you had patronised - the styles differed slightly, and old High School girls will remember that Kingswell's dresses were a paler blue. This photograph dates from 1957, and readers will perhaps remember that a little later Kingswell's expanded and for a time had a rather smart Viennese cafe on the upper floor.

Above: Lucky man, being able to join the birds on the tower of the Cathedral to view the north of the city! Below is the Bull Ring and that wide sweep of shops that flow into Northgate. In the distance is St John's Church in the Georgian square of the same name. The church is the central piece of the Square which is termed officially an 'out-of-town suburb.' The Cathedral itself, dedicated to All Saints, is the centre of the town, dominating the skyline literally with the spire seventy-five metres high. There has been a church on the site since Roman times and now the space around it adds to the sense of dignity

CLOSED 3/2011

Events of the 1930s

MELODY MAKERS
Throughout the 1930s a young American trombonist called Glenn Miller was making his mark in the world of music. By 1939 the Glenn Miller sound was a clear leader in the field; his clean-cut, meticulously executed arrangements of numbers such as 'A String of Pearls' and 'Moonlight Serenade' brought him fame across the world as a big-band leader. During a flight to England from Paris in 1944 Miller's plane disappeared; no wreckage was ever found.

THE WORLD AT LARGE
In India, Gandhi's peaceful protests against British rule were gathering momentum. The Salt Laws were a great bone of contention: forced to buy salt from the British government, thousands of protestors marched to the salt works, intending to take it over in the name of the Indian people. Policemen and guards attacked the marchers, but not one of them fought back. Gandhi, who earned for himself the name 'Mahatma' - Great Soul - was assassinated in 1948.

INVENTION AND TECHNOLOGY
With no driving tests or speed restrictions, 120,000 people were killed on the roads in Britain between the two world wars. In 1934 Percy Shaw invented a safety device destined to become familiar the world over: reflecting roadstuds. In dark or foggy conditions the studs that reflected light from the car's headlights kept traffic on the 'straight and narrow' and must over the years have saved many lives.

The shadow of All Saints Cathedral falls on the Bull Ring in this photograph taken in September 1953. The church of St John stands out in the background and interestingly there is in that part of Wakefield, though not visible here, the Roman Catholic Church of St Austin in Wentworth Terrace. This too is an imposing building, though not in the same style as St John's. The new bus station here had been open for a year at the time, and the bus station clock was

to become famous. This was the meeting place if you had a 'date'. How many romances in the 1950s and 60s, or even later, began with the faltering steps of a young beau in his gear getting off the bus, anxious not to appear too keen but dreading it if he was 'stood up'? Plenty of picture houses in the area for that first date as well. This vantage point today would afford a much different view of the Bull Ring and the surrounding buildings. The Ring has for very good reasons lost its shape. It appears to have been side-lined and has lost that sense of space it seems to possess here in this photograph. Traffic has been the main reason for that and for much of the other changes to town and city centres over the years.

Above: A young mum takes advantage of a gap in the traffic to shepherd her family safely across the road. This view of the Springs was taken in June 1970, and in spite of the huge increase in the number of cars on the road, restricted access to the Springs makes it easier for the mothers of today to cross here.

The design of baby carriages has changed a lot in the last 30 years. The pram wheeled by this young mum looks very much like one of those produced by Silver Cross. If so, this would be a lucky baby. The last word in luxury, Silver Cross made it their aim to produce 'the finest there is among baby carriages', and for many years a Rolls Royce car - comparable in quality - featured in their advertisements. The company's founder was William Wilson, a perambulator springsmith, who in 1877 set up in business in Silver Cross Street, Leeds, manufacturing prams. By the late 1990s Silver Cross were producing around 30,000 prams of all types at their factory in Guiseley.

Above right: We have become so used to today's attitude to tobacco advertising that blatant ads such as the Players sign on the railway bridge over Kirkgate now seem rather shocking.
The little tobacconist next door to the White Swan carries an amazing number of adverts for cigarettes and tobacco, and it comes as quite a shock today to be told that Players please or that you're never alone with a Strand, or to be advised to buy Wills Cut Golden Bar or Capstan full strength. Society likes to think of itself as being educated regarding such issues as lung cancer, heart disease and hardening arteries, and in more recent years advertisers have found themselves in the position of having to respond to new laws which make it necessary to declare the dangers of smoking cigarettes. But even as recently as 1960, the year of the photograph, nobody worried much about it. It was 1971 before cigarette advertising and packets were required to carry a government health warning on the dangers of smoking.

Below: This was Kirkgate in April 1971, and a keen eye will spot that this bus bound for Eastmoor Estate bears a Derbyshire registration. By the late 1960s many of Wakefield's fleet had become unreliable and 974 ARA was one of 82 vehicles purchased from other bus companies. In the background of the photograph, 'Monte Walsh', starring Lee Marvin, was showing at the ABC cinema. Slated by critics as one of the most boring westerns ever made, the film slid unnoticed into obscurity. The luxurious 1,700-seat cinema first opened in the mid 1930s as The Regal, and the manager's introduction of continuous performances - a real innovation at the time - made it a serious rival to all other Wakefield cinemas. The silver screen in the living room led to declining audiences in the 1950s and 60s, but the Regal was given a new lease of life in November 1976, when it opened as the ABC triple cinema. Sadly, this too was to pass away and by the beginning of the new millennium the building stood silent and empty.

The Regal was given a new lease of life in November 1976 - opening as the ABC triple cinema

At the time of this picture the Corn Exchange still stood in Westgate

Spot the landmark in this aerial view of the city - and then play 'spot the difference'! The Town Hall, in the foreground, is easily picked out, as is the West Riding Court House nearby, and the tower of the County Hall in the left corner of the picture. From there, Northgate carries the eye upwards towards the Bull Ring and on to the Cathedral, whose majestic steeple dwarfs the surrounding buildings. To its left we can spot the rooftops of the open market and the old market hall. On the far right of the view we can see that the Corn Exchange still stood in Westgate at the time of the photograph. The bus station had yet to be built, however; how many of our readers were at the enormous bonfire which was held on its site near the Bull Ring to celebrate the end of World War II? Guy Fawkes would not have been sitting atop the fire on this particular bonfire night; did someone make an effigy of Herr Hitler for the occasion, we wonder?

Like a three-dimensional map, the city centre, with its lofty Cathedral spire pointing heavenwards, lies spread out below us. To the right of the Cathedral, the Vicar's Croft burial ground, where nearly 150 victims of cholera were buried in the 1800s, has now been cleared for redevelopment; the Springs has been widened, and the new market hall is in the process of construction. Three gas holders to the right of the photograph remind us of the source of power that was introduced to Wakefield early in the 19th century. The Wakefield Gas Light Company in Vicarage Road was founded in 1822, providing a

comparatively brilliant source of street and domestic lighting, plus heat, power, and other commodities we tend to forget about, such as coke, tar for our roads and products for use in artificial manure and cleaning solutions. The grounds of Stanley Royd hospital - at one time known as simply 'The Asylum' - just creep into the top right of the photograph.

Events of the 1940s

HOT OFF THE PRESS
At the end of World War II in 1945 the Allies had their first sight of the unspeakable horrors of the Nazi extermination camps they had only heard of until then. In January, 4,000 emaciated prisoners more dead than alive were liberated by the Russians from Auschwitz in Poland, where three million people, most of them Jews,were murdered. The following year 23 prominent Nazis faced justice at Nuremberg; 12 of them were sentenced to death for crimes against humanity.

THE WORLD AT LARGE
The desert area of Alamogordo in New Mexico was the scene of the first atomic bomb detonation on July 16, 1945. With an explosive power equal to more than 15,000 tons of TNT, the flash could be seen 180 miles away. President Truman judged that the bomb could secure victory over Japan with far less loss of US lives than a conventional invasion, and on 6th August the first of the new weapons was dropped on Hiroshima. Around 80,000 people died.

ROYAL WATCH
By the end of World War II, the 19-year-old Princess Elizabeth and her distant cousin Lieutenant Philip Mountbatten RN were already in love. The King and Queen approved of Elizabeth's choice of husband, though they realised that she was rather young and had not mixed with many other young men. The engagement announcement was postponed until the Princess had spent four months on tour in Africa. The couple's wedding on 20th November 1947 was a glittering occasion - the first royal pageantry since before the war.

High rise blocks, such as Carr House Flats, began to rise skyward early in the 1960s

The 1960s saw the transforming of a way of life for many whose homes had lacked indoor toilets and baths, and for some families the only way - quite literally - was up. High rise blocks such as Carr House flats, just off George Street, began to rise skywards early in the decade, and Carr House, seen towards the bottom left in this view, was ready for its first occupants in 1961. The Regal Cinema in Kirkgate (centre foreground) delighted audiences for many years. The Ridings centre eventually replaced many of the buildings in the centre of the photograph, though it has over the course of time established its own particular character. Its choice of 90 or so shops gives us the opportunity to get inside out of the rain and browse among our favourite stores in warmth and comfort! To the right of the photograph, the new market hall stands out among the older buildings like Santa Claus in July. Nearby, the bus station was by this time up and running.

This changing city

Waiting for a bus was a way of life back in the 1920s when owning a motor car was a far off dream for the ordinary person in the street; the alternatives were pedal power or Shanks' pony! The beautiful old Morris standing in The Springs - almost unrecognisable in this early view - undoubtedly belonged to one of our more affluent citizens. But for those stuck in a bus queue there was often the possibility of buying an ice cream (known locally, for some obscure reason, as 'okey-pokey') from the vendor whose usual position was in the doorway recess of the Conservative Club wall on the right. The gaily painted ice cream carts were a familiar sight around Wakefield at the time, and most of the vendors were Italian. Just pulling into the second stand is bus number HL 2030, part of a new batch of 38 purchased by the West Riding Automobile Company in 1924. Enthusiasts will enjoy reading that the 20-seat buses, with Bristol built coachwork, were numbered 163-200, HL 1006-2043.

This page: Many local people felt very strongly that the old market should have stayed, and for them it was a sad day when the bulldozers moved in to begin their demolition in the summer of 1962, exactly 111 years after it was built *(bottom)*. The gaily-striped canvas covers of the open market can be seen in the background of the photograph, and as the workmen moved into the market hall the traders moved out. Disruption, however, was minimal as they were able to carry on selling from stalls in the open market. Interestingly, the flat caps worn by the men clearing the site and loading up the lorries were the hardest hats around. 'No hat, no boots, no job' is the slogan that reflects today's emphasis on workers' safety, but 40 years ago employees undertook many dangerous jobs every day without gauntlets, safety glasses, hard hats or protective clothing of any kind, and reflected very little on the risk factor. In fact, in some

occupations it was regarded as being somewhat less than macho to wear protective clothing. Viewed from Westmorland Street before the main market hall was demolished, the building still retains much of its original character *(left)*. The fine old building saw its grand opening on 29th August 1851, and whether you wanted a second hand coat or a cauliflower, Wakefield market was where you would find it. Wakefield has had its markets since 1204, and long before this building was constructed it had established itself as the place to find a bargain. A man once bought a wife here back in the 19th century, though history is silent on whether or not the lady turned out to be a bargain!

Looking up Northgate in Festival of Britain year, 1951, at buildings which were and still are part of the life of Wakefield, the Strafford Arms Hotel and the Talbot and Falcon Public House. The latter is recognisable, the former you need to go round the corner now to view. The hunting picture of a talbot dog and falcon seems a little out of place in a city centre but the pub has retained its tradi-tional name at least in an age when pub names have taken on a new style. Think of how many pubs in Wakefield exist with new titles. The New Dolphin had a more welcoming resonance to it than its present title. Up from the Talbot and Falcon are the remains of Cantor's furniture shop at one time belonging to Bleasbys. Two very interesting British cars here are the Morris 8 and in

front a Wolseley. The latter, like Riley, produced up-market cars. Later Riley Elf and the Wolseley Hornet would have a more distinctive ring to them than just plain Austin Mini which was introduced into this country in 1959. At this time Wolseley stood on its own as part of a booming British car industry. These were the times when Hillman, Austin, Morris, Lanchester and many more with Fords were generally the only cars on the roads of this country.

Events of the 1940s

MELODY MAKERS
The songs of radio personalities such as Bing Crosby and Vera Lynn were whistled, sung and hummed everywhere during the 1940s. The 'forces' sweetheart' brought hope to war-torn Britain with 'When the Lights go on Again', while the popular crooner's 'White Christmas' is still played around Christmas time even today. Who can forget songs like 'People Will Say we're in Love', 'Don't Fence Me In', 'Zip-a-dee-doo-dah', and 'Riders in the Sky'?

INVENTION AND TECHNOLOGY
Inspired by quick-drying printers' ink, in 1945 Hungarian journalist Laszlo Biro developed a ballpoint pen which released viscous ink from its own reservoir as the writer moved the pen across the page. An American inventor was working on a similar idea at the same time, but it was Biro's name that stuck. A few years later Baron Bich developed a low cost version of the pen, and the 'Bic' ballpoint went on sale in France in 1953.

SCIENCE AND DISCOVERY
In 1943 Ukrainian-born biochemist Selman Abraham Waksman made a significant discovery. While studying organisms found in soil he discovered an antibiotic (a name Waksman himself coined) which was later found to be the very first effective treatment for tuberculosis. A major killer for thousands of years, even the writings of the ancient Egyptians contain stories of people suffering from tuberculosis. Waksman's development of streptomycin brought him the 1952 Nobel Prize for Medicine.

Above: The old brick fronted Market Hall looks down on the excavations of the area at the junction of Brook Street and Westmorland Street - this was the beginning of a new market for Wakefield. The idea of markets, once the very heart of shopping and commerce, still continues today. Shoppers are fascinated by them. The present Victorian Market held in November has spread its wings to the paved areas around the Cathedral into Teall Street, All Saints Walk and the Cathedral Precinct - almost back to its roots and to the sixteenth century description which stated 'Wakefield upon Calder is a very quick market town, well served of flesh and fish from the sea and rivers, so that a right honest man shall fare well for 2d a meal'. Nothing has changed except the price. What has changed is the nineteenth century practice of selling your wife at Wakefield market. Otherwise the range of products on offer is still wide.

Above right: This scene enacted in the Bull Ring in March 1966 was a familiar one which had been repeated around Wakefield since the early 1950s. The little knot of passers-by on the left take no notice as yet another of the city's old buildings is transformed into bricks and rubble. They had seen it all before, and as the new concrete and glass construction rose above the fragments of the old they would once more raise their eyebrows, shrug their shoulders - and get on with getting used to it. To the right of the photograph, Kathy's Cafe today offers coffee, tea, or a substantial meal to weary shoppers. Readers will perhaps remember the night club which once offered refreshment of a quite different kind. Its claim to infamy, according to a number of indignant punters who patronised the establishment, was that the management charged you for a glass of water! The curve of the building which was at the time Kingswells outfitters can be seen in the background; future years would see its use changed to banking; eventually the building and indeed the whole block would be extensively modernised.

The beginning of the end for the Grand Electric Cinema and the other businesses in this reminder of Wakefield's past. The cinema industry had gone into a period of decline by the time this photograph was taken in August 1963. Television became the staple entertainment and Housey Housey became Bingo and a national pastime. In 1960 the cinema audiences in this country had fallen by two-thirds compared to the early 1950s. Gimmicks like 3-D with those green and red cardboard glasses and Cinemascope had been introduced to lure people away from their television sets; spectacular films such as 'The Ten Commandments' and 'West Side Story', however popular, could not stop the tide. There were too many cinemas for a declining demand. The Grand Electric was to suffer like so many others. Its other name of the 'Ranch' epitomised its decline. Westerns were all right when we did not have 'The Lone Ranger' and 'Rawhide' in our front room on a weekly basis, but with the increasing popularity of commercial television why pay to go to the cinema when you could stay at home and watch TV for nothing?

If this fine building had not been demolished in 1963, would it have survived through the subsequent years and become part of Wakefield's architectural heritage? It was a part of the city's history; it did play a significant role in the city's commercial life as it prospered in the nineteenth century. But its presence by this time appeared to

be a confusion of differing purposes. It was probably considered to have outlived its usefulness. As Wakefield responded to the country's increasing prosperity in the 1960s when we were told by the then Prime Minister, Harold Macmillan, that we had never had it so good, town centre redevelopment took on a new impetus. The old was

beginning to be replaced by new shops, nationally owned, who could sell more and at a cheaper cost to a more demanding public. There was no need for the old Grand Electric. There was a need for new types of businesses which reflected contemporary consumer needs and demands. Had that old building survived past 1963, would it have stumbled on for a few more years until another redevelopment scheme found no use for it?

Events of the 1950s

WHAT'S ON?
Television hit Britain in a big way during the 1950s. Older readers will surely remember 'Double Your Money, Dixon of Dock Green and 'Dragnet' (whose characters' names were changed 'to protect the innocent'). Commercial television was introduced on 22nd September 1955, and Gibbs SR toothpaste were drawn out of the hat to become the first advert to be shown. Many believed adverts to be vulgar, however, and audiences were far less than had been hoped for.

GETTING AROUND
The year 1959 saw the development of the world's first practical air-cushion vehicle - better known to us as the hovercraft. The earliest model was only able to travel at slow speeds over very calm water and was unable to carry more than three passengers. The faster and smoother alternative to the sea ferry quickly caught on, and by the 1970s a 170-ton car-carrying hovercraft service had been introduced across the English Channel.

SPORTING CHANCE
The four-minute mile had remained the record since 1945, and had become regarded as virtually unbreakable. On 6th May 1954, however, Oxford University student Roger Bannister literally ran away with the record, accomplishing the seemingly impossible in three minutes 59.4 seconds. Bannister collapsed at the end of his last amazing lap, even temporarily losing his vision. By the end of the day, however, he had recovered sufficiently to celebrate his achievement in a London night club!

There was so little traffic about on the day this scene was caught on camera that there seemed little need for these shoppers to use the zebra crossing. The people of Britain got their first pedestrian crossings, marked out by studs and yellow beacons, back in 1934. The first beacons were made of glass and made a wonderful target for little boys with stones, so the glass beacons were replaced by painted aluminium globes. Crossings got their stripes in 1951, and the beacons became

The people of Britain got their first pedestrian crossings back in 1934

plastic and began to wink in 1952.

The photograph dates from March 1966, and as we can see, the city centre was still enduring the onslaughts of the bulldozer. The origins of Lewis P Hughes' wine merchants and grocery business go back as far as 1785. When the building housing their 'Italian Warehouse' in the Bull Ring was demolished, the business was moved to these temporary premises until the new store, built on the site of the old one, was ready for occupation.

A helping hand

What the Wakefield branch of the WVS did when its help was needed urgently could well be summed up in the one word often used to describe that organisation - undaunted. The ways these ladies came to join WVS are varied. Lillian Ziegler, front right in this photograph, thought she was going gardening when she was 'volunteered'. She never looked back and served from 1958 until 1982. She was one of many. As we can see here, the national appeals for clothing for all kinds of reasons bought a magnificent response from the ladies of the WVS and from the public. The members took it upon themselves to co-ordinate the efforts. Whether it was the Lynmouth Disaster, the floods on the East Coast or the massive influx of refugees in 1956 from Hungary or in 1961 from the island of Tristan de Cunha, threatened by a volcano, the WVS was never found wanting. Clothes always poured in. We can see here Lillian Ziegler, Mary Strafford and Margaret Taylor sorting the clothing out before it was packed into bales, ready for transporting. Whatever the refugees would have thought of some of the clothing brought in we do not know but ball gowns and evening dresses and suits were not really appropriate. No doubt the ladies of the WVS would find some use for them - they were like that. They always had to have a stock of clothing for no-one was to know when they would be called on again either for a local family or for others caught up in some catastrophe.

Events of the 1950s

HOT OFF THE PRESS
The 1950s seemed to be the heyday of spies, and in 1951 the activities of Guy Burgess and Donald Maclean caused a sensation in the country. Both had occupied prominent positions in the Foreign Office, while Burgess had also been a member of MI-6. Recruited by the Russians while at Cambridge University in the 1930s, the traitors provided the Soviets with a huge amount of valuable information. They disappeared in 1951, surfacing in Moscow five years later.

THE WORLD AT LARGE
Plans to develop the economies of member states into one common market came to fruition on 1st January 1958, when the EEC came into operation. The original members were France, Belgium, Luxembourg, The Netherlands, Italy, and West Germany. The Community became highly successful, achieving increased trade and prosperity across Western Europe while at the same time alleviating fear of war which lingered on after the end of World War II. Britain became a member in 1973.

SCIENCE AND DISCOVERY
DNA (deoxyribonucleic acid) was first defined as long ago as 1953, and the effects have been far-reaching. The key discovery was developed over the following years and today DNA fingerprinting has become an accepted part of life. Genetic diseases such as hemophilia and cystic fibrosis have been identified. Criminals are continually detected and brought to justice. Biological drugs have been developed. More controversially, drought and disease-resistant plants have been engineered - and Dolly the sheep has been produced.

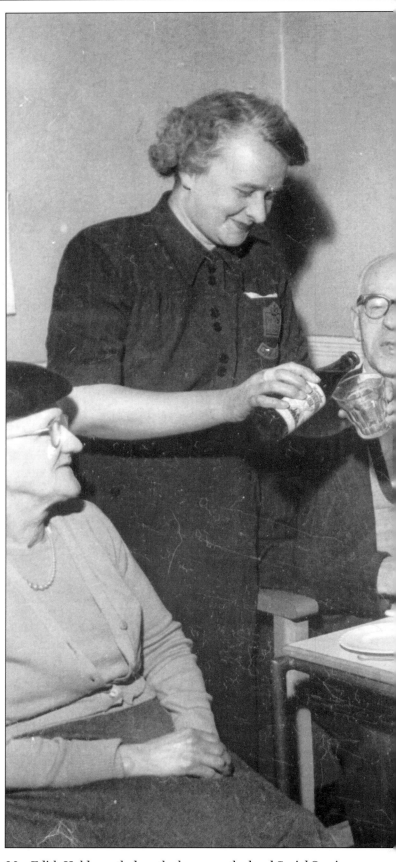

Mrs Edith Holdsworth does the honours, the local Social Services Director acts as waiter and the toast is 'Cheers! Happy Christmas' at the 1959 Christmas party for members of the Women's Voluntary Service Luncheon Club held in its headquarters under the Music Saloon in what is now the Wakefield Museum. The Luncheon club, a kind of spin off from the Meals on Wheels Service, instigated nationally in 1948, was only one of many activities of that organi-

sation. Having been set up in 1938 as war threatened, its first Chairman was the redoubtable Marchioness of Reading. The work those members did during the dark days of war was memorable and often nothing short of heroic. After the war the WVS was given two years to live - it has been a long two years. Think of Rose Hips, the afore-mentioned Meals on Wheels and many more activities where help and volunteers were needed often as matter of urgency and that is the WVS. So pour the drinks, have a good meal, enjoy yourselves and there is entertainment to come. There is carol singing and WVS members will do their party pieces, including their version of Flanagan and Allan, fur coats and all. All together now - 'Underneath the Arches, down Paradise Way....'

Bottom: A visit to WVS headquarters by the Mayor was a recognition of the valuable work the ladies readily undertook. This particular one was to view the giant knitted patchwork blanket, another task which challenged the skills and ingenuity of the members. Here Adele Simpson, now Hill, Edith Holdsworth and Barbara Whittaker show off their finished product. The other activities undertaken by the members over the years are varied. Think of hospital trolleys and out-patients' services and rest rooms; the WVS work in 1328 hospitals and clinics; its national car service has served 300,000 patients covering three million miles. Members have worked with the Armed Services in times of war; they had established at one time twenty national food flying squads. That is why there was a party at Buckingham Palace and a service in Westminster Abbey in 1959 to celebrate its coming of age. That is why the Women's Voluntary Service was allowed to add 'Royal' to its name in 1966. Local members went to York to celebrate before another service of thanksgiving was later held in Westminster Abbey attended by its original patron, the present Queen Mother. And that is the reason ladies like Edith Holdsworth and Lillian Ziegler were given MBEs in recognition of their services to the WVS. All will recall their days with fond memories of service, friendship and not a little fun. The motto, 'Not why we can't, But how we can', is a fitting tribute to them all.

Right: The threat of another war after 1945 was never far from this country's mind as it vowed it would never again be so unprepared as it was in 1939. The emphasis was now on Civil Defence and the Armed Forces and the police, the fire service and the medical and nursing services were central to this. Exercises were regularly held and it was the job of the WVS to set up feeding stations. Enjoying a well earned cuppa on this occasion with members of the local fire brigade are from left to right are Edith Holdsworth, Mrs Simpson, Mrs Coates, Mary Freeman and Lillian Ziegler. Cooking meals for the participants in these exercises involved making an oven from bricks and clay. Making the pug for the clay was a messy business and usually the job of a very meticulous lady who hated getting her hands dirty. The more she expressed her hatred for this job, the more she was asked to do it. She soon grew to love it! So did the other ladies for they were usually to be found setting up their feeding stations near the Old Sewerage Works and the smell grew on them, often literally. Like the lady with the pug they remembered that later with a certain affection. What they may have said and thought at the time has been conveniently forgotten.

On the move

> *By 1932 trams had become unpopular, and the authorities decided to replace them with motor buses*

Younger readers who are used to seeing green buses around Wakefield might be surprised if we were to have this photograph available in colour. Vehicle HL 5323 was one of the fleet of 48 Leyland Titan TD2 motor buses which were purchased to replace the old trams - and their livery was red, echoing the original colour of the tramcars. The bus is pictured outside the Leeds Crossgates carriage works of Charles Roe, who built the 48-seat, centre entrance, bodies. Note the cranking handle in situ on the vehicle, and imagine trying to start the bus engine with it! The handle was only used if the battery was flat, in which case a rope would be tied to it and three men would apply the required muscle-power.

It was 1932, and the switch from trams to motor buses moved public transport forward in Wakefield. By 1930, the picturesque though draughty old trams had already become unpopular with the travelling public, and in spite of the massive costs involved (£180,000), the authorities decided to scrap them. The outdated old vehicles were therefore dispatched to that great tramshed in the sky, and on 25th July 1932 the very last tram ran on the Ossett to Agbrigg route.

Buses have long acted as mobile advertisement hoardings, and trams before them, and here the passers-by are being encouraged to buy Talbot's popular sweets. This view of Northgate and the Bull Ring dates from 1949, the year that sweet rationing came to an end in Britain and the children of Wakefield could buy as many bags of Talbot's as their pocket money would allow. Their joy, however, was short-lived, and hearts sank when after a few months sweets rationing was re-introduced. It was 1954 before the day arrived which the entire nation had been waiting for; crowds of people who were sick and tired of coupons gathered in Trafalgar Square and

joyfully tore up their much-hated ration books.
The roads were particularly busy when the photographer snapped this view from the middle of the road, and we are left wondering whether he became part of Wakefield's accident statistics! The road sweeper on the left, armed with brush and shovel, reminds us of the way the job used to be done before today's suction cleaners were invented.

Events of the 1950s

MELODY MAKERS
Few teenage girls could resist the blatant sex-appeal of 'Elvis the Pelvis', though their parents were scandalised at the moody Presley's provocatively gyrating hips. The singer took America and Britain by storm with such hits as 'Jailhouse Rock', 'All Shook Up' and 'Blue Suede Shoes'. The rhythms of Bill Haley and his Comets, Buddy Holly and Chuck Berry turned the 1950s into the Rock 'n' Roll years.

INVENTION AND TECHNOLOGY
Until the late 1950s you did not carry radios around with you. Radios were listened to at home, plugged into a mains socket in every average sitting room. Japan was in the forefront of electronic developments even then, and in 1957 the Japanese company Sony introduced the world's very first all-transistor radio - an item of new technology that was small enough to fit into your pocket. The major consumer product caught on fast - particularly with teenage listeners.

ROYAL WATCH
King George VI's health had been causing problems since 1948, when he developed thrombosis. In 1951 the King - always a heavy smoker - became ill again, and was eventually found to be suffering from lung cancer. His left lung was removed in September of 1951. In January 1952 he waved Princess Elizabeth and Prince Philip off on their tour of Africa; they were never to see him again. The King died in the early hours of 6th February 1952.

Above: Ready for action - this fully equipped bus conductor looks anxious but ready for anything as he poses in front of his AEC Regent double decker. The scene is set at the bottom of the Springs with the corner of the Cathedral visible in the background. The driver, on the right, looks more casual, doubtless thinking that he was 'out of shot' as the photographer performed his art. Records show the vehicle was delivered in November 1946 as an addition to the tram replacement fleet. The vehicle was originally painted red, but the colour was changed to green in December 1954 due to a shortage of vehicles on the local 'green' routes. The bus was withdrawn in 1960 and scrapped a year later.

Above right: In September 1952 Wakefield got the new bus station for which the travelling public had waited for ever since the land was acquired before the second world war. Snapped at their new terminus, two of Wakefield's red buses are ready to pick up their passengers. The front vehicle was almost a veteran of the fleet, being one of five Leyland Titan buses purchased in 1936.

Those boarding the AEC Regent bus on the right would do well to check both destination blinds and to consult the driver as well, who was the deciding factor in the argument about whether the bus was on route Number 11 or 12. We have no doubt that passengers eventually arrived safely at their destination, which was in the end all that really mattered. Between 1946 and 1949, 62 vehicles were acquired to replace the ageing 1932 fleet; this vehicle, BHL 343, was one of them.

Below: The travelling public had to get used to a whole new way of paying fares when the first one-man operated buses came into service. This was 1961, and the very first of the new-style, 41-seat buses, still bearing that gleaming 'brand new' look, was captured for posterity as it passed through the Bull Ring on its way to the bus station. A total of 12 AFC Reliance, dual-door single deckers were added to West Riding's fleet. Letting the good old conductors go, however, was to have a good news/bad news 'swings and roundabouts' effect; the good news - as far as West Riding was concerned - was of course that one man could now do the job of two. The bad news was that it took longer for passengers to board the bus and find a seat - and also there was now only one person to take all the flak from disgruntled or aggressive passengers. However, the new system was adopted and today paying the driver has simply become part of life.

Bottom: This photograph is bound to appeal to railway enthusiasts and nostalgia buffs of all ages. The once-familiar clock above Westgate Station, removed in a previous round of 'improvements', is sadly missed by travellers who caught their trains by it - and locals who once set their watches by its hourly strike. As 1999 ended and the new millennium began, further major modernisation was on the cards to cope with the increasing popularity of the station. The age of steam is represented in this nostalgic view by the mighty ADDAX, number 61014, from a design first seen in 1942. It weighed a hefty 71 tons. This class of engine was phased out between 1962 and 1967.

Thick winter coats, warm boots, scarves and mufflers, hats and gloves - all the trappings of a chilly January day can be seen among the passengers queuing for the Sandal bus - and very thankful they would be, too, when they managed to find themselves a seat in the comparative warmth of the West Riding public transport! Were those at the back of the queue perhaps wondering whether there would be enough room for them on the bus? From our viewpoint we can see, however, that there were plenty of seats left

Events of the 1960s

WHAT'S ON?
Television comedy came into its own in the 1960s, and many of the shows that were favourites then went on to become classics. 'On the Buses', 'Steptoe and Son', 'Till Death Us Do Part' and 'The Army Game' kept audiences laughing, while the incredible talents of Morecambe and Wise, the wit of Des O'Connor - often the butt of the duo's jokes - and the antics of Benny Hill established them for ever in the nation's affections.

GETTING AROUND
The 2nd March 1969 was a landmark in the history of aviation. The Anglo-French supersonic airliner Concorde took off for the first time from Toulouse in France. Concorde, which can cruise at almost twice the speed of sound, was designed to fly from London to New York in an incredible three hours twenty minutes. The event took place just weeks after the Boeing 747, which can carry 500 passengers to Concorde's modest 100, made its first flight.

SPORTING CHANCE
Wembley Stadium saw scenes of jubilation when on 30th July 1966 England beat West Germany 4-2 in the World Cup. The match, played in a mixture of sunshine and showers, had been a nailbiting experience for players and spectators alike from the very beginning when Germany scored only thirteen minutes into the game. It was Geoff Hurst's two dramatic goals scored in extra time that secured the victory and lifted the cup for England - at last.

on the upper deck. And even if you were a non-smoker (a rarity at the time) you would opt to put up with other people's smoke for a while rather than hang around with frozen feet, waiting for the next bus. After all, there was not the same knowledge in the 1940s about the health risks of passive smoking.

Self-service filling stations were just making an appearance in the 1960s

De-coking your engine was a way of life back in the 1960s, especially if you were a motor-bike owner, and Burrows motor cycle and car dealer was the place to go for your Redex. It's many years since drivers were allowed to park on the pavement and fill their tank via this kind of petrol pipe on a swinging arm. And a good thing, too, safety-conscious readers will add. How many remember filling up at Burrows' Newbridge Garage in the days when they drove their own Morris Minor? Is the gentleman in the picture Mr Burrows himself, we wonder? Self-serve filling stations were only just being introduced at the time, and many readers will remember with nostalgia the time when you could drive your car into a petrol station and not only have the services of attendants who filled up your tank, but who also cleaned your windscreen and asked if you needed oil. In 1960 petrol was four and sevenpence halfpenny a gallon (was the word 'litre' in the English dictionary?), though a year later the price rose by a further threepence owing to an increase in purchase tax.

Shopping spree

This page: Teall Street was buzzing with life when a photographer captured the scene one market day in July 1960 *(bottom)*. Already many of the ladies in the scene (two or three of them with reluctant hubbies in tow), are heading homewards with bulging bags and baskets over their arms. Buying potatoes and tomatoes from one stall, apples and sprouts from another and perhaps cabbage and a couple of grapefruit from a third have always been part of the fun of bargain hunting among the fruit and veg stalls.

Cheerful, noisy and lively are words which aptly describe the open markets; they would have made a good starting place for a lot of local housewives, who week after week would catch a bus into town and browse from stall to stall to find the best - and cheapest - fresh food, clothes for the children (and themselves), bags and purses, books and magazines, and much more. As we look across the many-ridged covers over the open stalls, shopping bags were beginning to fill up when this view was caught on camera *(below left)*. Shopping lists in hand, the housewives of Wakefield pick things up, put them down again, decide whether to buy or not. The subject uppermost in their minds is likely to be concerned with deciding whether to spec out and buy a cauliflower, or to stick with cabbage (cheaper, perhaps, though perhaps less popular with the children!) to go with their Sunday roast this week. A trip to the meat and fish market for their pork chops and Sunday joint might follow, and whether her family liked kippers for breakfast or fish cakes for tea, the housewife was spoilt for choice. The prices charged by markets and street traders have traditionally been a few coppers cheaper than the average high street greengrocer would charge, and a weekly walk around the market could save a shilling or two here and there, and stretch the inadequate housekeeping money a little bit further.

Two-way traffic on the Springs, a Morris 8 and a Morris van, a Scammel railway van delivering parcels and a picnic on a traffic island. Or is he having a rest or been told to 'Wait there, I won't be long'? The Springs is a different place today. It is now restricted to buses only. The shape is the same though as we look down from Westmorland Street towards Lower Warrengate and Vicarage Street

which now takes all the traffic round the rear of the Market past the Labour Club where Young Socialist Discos used to 'happen' in a little red (appropriately) hut. The businesses remain with different emphases. The Indian Restaurant remains but the rest of that block has not that vitality today. Above there will be less vitality and more scrutiny as an inconspicuous sign states that the upper storeys are

dedicated to HM Customs and Excise. The shops above that block have all changed. In this photograph they are busy and look well established with some well known names of today. Wakefield's first supermarket, Carlin's, was situated here. It is a pity that today there are so many shops empty here. Shopping centres are more attractive and small businesses generally move into them, or struggle, or close. A sign of the times.

Events of the 1960s

HOT OFF THE PRESS
Barbed wire, concrete blocks and a wide no-man's-land divided East from West when a reinforced wall was built right across the city of Berlin in 1961. Many East Germans escaped to the West at the eleventh hour, taking with them only the possessions they could carry. The Berlin Wall divided the city - and hundreds of family members and friends - for 28 years until the collapse of Communist rule across Eastern Europe. Who can ever forget those scenes in 1989, when ordinary people themselves began to physically tear down the hated wall?

THE WORLD AT LARGE
'One giant leap for mankind' was taken on 20th July 1969, when Neil Armstrong made history as the first man to set foot on the moon. During the mission he and fellow-astronaut 'Buzz' Aldrin collected rock and soil samples, conducted scientific experiments - and had a lot of fun jumping around in the one-sixth gravity. Twenty-one hours and thirty-seven minutes after their landing they took off again in their lunar module 'Eagle' to rejoin Apollo II which was orbiting above them, proudly leaving the American flag on the Moon's surface.

ROYAL WATCH
Princess Margaret's announcement in 1960 that she was to wed photographer Antony Armstrong-Jones (later Lord Snowdon) brought sighs of relief from her immediate family. Just five years earlier the people of Britain had sympathised as the princess bowed to public and private pressure, ending her relationship with Peter Townsend, Prince Philip's former equerry. The Church (and the Queen, as its Head) frowned on the liaison as Townsend was divorced. Her marriage to Lord Snowdon itself ended in 1978.

Below: TheBull Ring in 1958 is crowded with pedestrians. The two cars in the scene do not appear to be a threat to anyone, especially as there are now safe areas to cross. Zebra crossings were once described as a 'walker's magic carpet'. It will not be long before the magic has gone to be replaced by something more sinister. Traffic, private and commercial, will increase at an alarming rate within the next ten years. Traffic wardens had already been introduced to town and city centres, slightly different from today's version. The original proposal was that they should be 'non-uniformed patrols enlisted from the ranks of ex-police officers, time expired servicemen and others who might welcome a part-time job to add to their pension'. New parking schemes were introduced, the forerunners of the modern single and double yellow lines. Parking meters, each of which was estimated to earn an average of £35 per year, would pay for the cost of providing the wardens. Life was going to become very difficult for the motorist. MOT tests had been in force for some time; fines for breaking traffic laws and regulations were to be more severe, but in this picture all appears to be bliss - so far.

Right: It would appear that the only feature left today is the zebra crossing and the tops of the shops as we look from the Bull Ring towards the bus station, built in 1952. The names of the shops have changed; the Griffin Hotel now has another title. Even the lamp standards with those big heavy fluorescent tubes did not last long before they were replaced by sodium lighting. This is the period between the enlarging of the Bull Ring and the new developments. A model of the new Wakefield had been created for the Council by the City Engineer and Architect. The model was proved to be fairly accurate in its planning; the time to its completion for the people of Wakefield seemed to have lasted a generation. And quite naturally progress and development still continue as Wakefield like every other town and city responds to the changes in people's shopping and leisure habits, the demands of business and trade and traffic growth, and tries to seek a balance between meeting those needs and preserving that which is worth preserving. Hard decisions indeed and many different answers and solutions were no doubt on offer.

Bottom: Only our more mature readers will remember the Six Chimneys, which once stood on the corner of Kirkgate and Legh Street. The date of this ancient building is well recorded, as the year '1566' was carved on the main entrance and on the southern gable. At the centre of the building was a massive 16ft wide stone chimney into which six flues converged from its various fireplaces. This feature was important enough to give the building its name; back in the 16th century chimneys were built only into the homes of more affluent citizens, so this would have been its most remarkable feature.

By the 1920s the ground floor of Six Chimneys was being used as shops, and we can see from this view which dates from around 1922 that the beautiful old house was sadly showing its age. After all, the first Queen Elizabeth was on the throne when it was built! We can perhaps imagine what the building was like in its younger days, when its herring-bone panels and its fine oak staircases were new, and the Tudor hunting scenes carved on its timbers were fresh from the wood-carver's chisel. It was a sad day for Wakefield when, on the evening of 16th May 1941, its massive beams at last gave way to the ravages of time and Six Chimneys collapsed.

Right: There was a time when high streets around the country were sprinkled with an assortment of different shoe shops: Freeman, Hardy and Willis, Saxone, Dolcis, Timpson, Stead and Simpson, Barratts, Bata - there they all were. Is it imagination, or are there fewer shoe shops about today? Perhaps they all amalgamated.... William Simpson's extensive business was one of Wakefield's finest, and the display windows of his 'Shoe Corner' reached from Brook Street around the corner into Westmorland Street. More mature readers will surely remember shopping there for their Norvic or Mascot shoes in the 1930s and 40s. At the time of the photograph, this block of buildings was already lined up for demolition as part of the post war development of the Bull Ring. The shadowy figure of a passer-by, like a ghost from the past, reminds us of the Wakefield we once knew so well, and which was to vanish for ever.

Above: This is a photograph to stir memories of old Wakefield in 1952 as we look at the junction of Cross Square and Northgate and the entrance to Bread Street. The opening of the new bus station in 1952 bought an end to the old bus office next to Teale's grocery shop. It was now obsolete and soon it was to be demolished. It was here you could make bus enquiries, buy your tickets, collect your parcels and recover your lost property. Wakefield was just about to undergo development and shops and businesses like Hudson's, Brown's and Teale's, despite its offer of 'Better and Cheaper', were to become part of the past in the way of new shops and new initiatives. If we stand at this corner today it is hard to visualise the way things used to be. Wakefield seemed to be in a constant process of change. Soon after this photograph was taken, streets in the area were redeveloped and in the mid-1980s there was a second onslaught. The area does here look ripe for change however. Morton's faded announcement on its wall seems to reflect the mood - like the weather, bleak. These passers-by are more concerned with keeping warm rather than progress. And there was still rationing for her and her family; it was not until July 3rd 1954 that food rationing ended, although sweets came off in February 1952; white bread came back into the shops in the previous year, replacing the old National loaf and its price would be sixpence ha'penny. Times were still bleak. Any changes for the better were to be welcomed.

Top: How many readers remember the extraordinary time ball which was once mounted on Perkin's Shop? With workings too intricate and complicated for a lay person to understand, the ball of this amazing timepiece would fall at the designated hour. The kids loved it! This was the beginning of the restructuring of this area. It was May 1963 and Perkins was preparing to go, and no doubt these ladies were looking for bargains in all the shops. Out would go the old established locals, in would come fast foods, building societies and others meeting the contemporary customers' needs. Architecture would change too. The stonework and chimney pots would be replaced by more modern structures, designed for the times just like the ones we see here were designed for their time. Change is inevitable and in another generation when Church Square is redeveloped there may be some nostalgia about for the buildings erected here in the 1960s.

Was the Austin A40 on the left turquoise with a black roof, we wonder? This was by far the most popular colour with A40 owners. Often described as 'the first family hatchback', the Italian-designed motor was not, strictly speaking, a hatchback, but rather its forerunner. The boot could be accessed either from the back seat or from the rear. Our view up a very busy Teall Street towards its junction with The Springs in July 1970 from Upper Kirkgate gives us a glimpse of the old and the new. There are examples of the more modern fashions and one or two of the more traditional, particularly in the millinery department. There is the new Market Hall, completed in 1964, replacing the old building, and the relatively new 1904 extension to the Cathedral, dedicated to the memory of William Walsham How,

the first Bishop of Wakefield. New businesses have moved into the area and will dominate this and many other town centres. True-Form on the right was certainly not local but satisfied the consumers' demands for modern fashions at reasonable prices. It would be interesting to discover how many of the old high street shoe shops have survived and how many changes of ownership have taken place in this street since 1970 as shopping habits continue to change.

Events of the 1960s

MELODY MAKERS
The 1960s: those were the days when the talented blues guitarist Jimi Hendrix shot to rock stardom, a youthful Cliff Richard charmed the nation with his 'Congratulations' and Sandie Shaw won the Eurovision Song Contest for Britain with 'Puppet on a String'. It was the combined musical talents of a group of outrageous working-class Liverpool lads, however, who formed the Beatles and took the world by storm with music that ranged from the experimental to ballads such as 'Yesterday'.

INVENTION AND TECHNOLOGY
A major step forward was made in 1960 when the laser was invented. An acronym for Light Amplification by Stimulated Emission of Radiation, the device produces a narrow beam of light that can travel for vast distances and is focused to give enormous power. Laser beams, as well as being able to carry far more information than radio waves, can also be used for surgery, cutting, drilling, welding and scores of other operations.

SCIENCE AND DISCOVERY
When the drug Thalidomide was first developed during the 1950s it was hailed as a wonder drug which would ease the distressing symptoms of pregnancy sickness. By the early 1960s the drug's terrible side effects were being discovered, when more than 3000 babies had been born with severe birth defects. Malformed limbs, defective eyes and faulty intestines were the heart-rending legacy left by Thalidomide.

This page: More mature readers will be sure to remember the strange feeling of walking for the first time around a self service store with a wire basket over their arm, choosing their own goods from the shelves. It almost felt like stealing! Many shoppers will recall with nostalgia the days when they could ask their grocer for two pounds of sugar (remember the blue bags?), half a pound of bacon, a quarter of tea - and perhaps a couple of packets of crisps for the kids, always with a little blue bag of salt somewhere inside. The grocer would slice and weigh, cut and wrap, all the while chatting about the family, the war or the weather, with a personal service rarely seen in the impersonal supermarket of today. It really was like 'Open all Hours'! Those small self-service shops led quickly to the opening of the larger super-markets such as Fine Fare, Sainsbury's and Asda. Many smaller grocers went with the popular flow, supplying wire baskets and installing self-service units, but the new trend eventually resulted in the demise of many of Wakefield's corner shops. The supermarkets, however, were here to stay, and at the Queens Supermarket (which later became Asda), one little tot is using the railings as a climbing frame as she looks forward to a ride in her mum's trolley *(top)*. And untidy as the piled-up boxes undoubtedly were, it was a common practice for supermarkets to leave them for their customers. They came in very useful to carry home the shopping. Asda came into being in the early 1960s, when a number of companies with various interests - dairies, butchers, bakeries and cafe proprietors - joined forces to become Associated Dairies Ltd, which in its turn amalgamated with a firm of Yorkshire butchers. Asda - a combination of AS from 'Associated' and DA from 'Dairies' - opened this first Wakefield store in 1965.

Below: Remember the Bolenium overall shop and Army Stores? Stuffed to bursting point with an immense range of goods, this store in Teall Street - a modern clothes shop today - was pictured on November 4th 1955. It was the obvious port of call for any bloke who needed either working gear or casual clothes. Trousers, jackets, shirts, boots - you name it - if it was workwear - and you could almost certainly buy it here. The men gazing into the window might of course have been looking for a pair of jeans; if so, it would have been for their hard-wearing properties rather than for fashion. But a few years on denim jeans were destined to become the fashion of the decade - though they were in fact to remain popular right up to the end of the 1990s. Denim jeans were first introduced in the 19th century, when a factory in Nimes in France produced them as heavy duty workwear. Levi Strauss began to make jeans, mostly for gold mining. The familiar rivets which were part of the design began life as reinforcements to stop the weight of the gold nuggets tearing the pockets!

Bottom: The improvements to the Bull Ring as we can see here in 1951 meant the removal of the statue of Queen Victoria and the provision of an open space of flower beds and grassed surrounds. This roundabout with its 'Keep Left' signs, adequate at the time, gave useful information as to how to approach it. A pity one motorist seems to have disregarded it. Still, cycling appears to be a pleasure with more cycles than vehicles here. A bonus about this view from the tower of the Cathedral is, of course, what can be seen in the distance. Here we can see the old Stanley Royd Psychiatric Hospital. Times have changed and it is now closed. In the 1930s it only allowed daily visiting from 11am until 12 noon! We can see here the beginnings of the trend of the domination of town centres by non-local shops. How many of these businesses are national? They did sit easily in other parts of Wakefield with those locally owned and provided a balance. The imbalance was to occur very soon and as the consumers' habits and preferences changed so did the types of businesses. What is local here is the Beverley Brothers Brewery, famous for its 'Golden Eagle' ale from the Eagle Brewery in Harrison Street but not for long, unfortunately. By the 1960s it had suffered the fate of many a local brewery. Rationalisation was a term often used - swallowed up was a more accurate one.

purchasing horses and carts to deliver their goods, which had up to then been collected by the purchaser. Sadly, William Craven died in 1882, as did his wife Jane. However, in the same year Benjamin's son, Joe Henry joined the family firm where his brother William Holford had already been working for two years.

The business continued to flourish and by 1893 it had over a hundred employees. The brickmaking machinery, now well established, was beginning to find overseas markets and stiff plastic brickmaking machines were shipped off to South Africa, Germany, Italy Australia and Ireland. In 1898 the business became a Limited Company and John, Benjamin, John William and William Holford were made the first directors. At

around the same time Richard Parkinson Bradley's business failed and was put up for sale, allowing Bradley and Craven to purchase the firm for £10400.

Five years after the conversion to a Limited Company, John Craven died. The Roundwood Brickworks were sold leaving the firm, which now employed 300 people, to concentrate on sheet metal machinery, colliery winding engines, hauling gears, and clayworking machinery. By 1907 Bradley and Craven had purchased one of the first cars to appear on the roads of Wakefield. A year later William Holford Craven's son, Edward Stanley joined the business, eventually becoming Chairman in 1956!

In 1913, after serving as Chairman of the company for 11 years, Benjamin Craven died and was succeeded by John William. The advent of the first world war saw the Company established on the War Office and Admiralty lists' of suppliers. The firm's employees had to work night shifts to deal with the demands for their machines. After the war Bradley and Craven returned to its major industry, that of providing brick-making machinery. Joe Henry's son, Cyril Benjamin, joined the family business around this time as did William Holford's son, Wilfred Archer.

Left: The board of directors in 1963.
Below: An early view of the bay of the forge.

The business continued to thrive. Further extensions were carried out to the foundry and small machine shop in 1925, followed by alterations to the main office block in 1928 and extensions to the erecting shops in 1936. In 1938 trade in Scotland was so extensive that the need for a Scottish Depot became apparent. This depot was opened in Glasgow and proved to be of great benefit to the many firms in the North who operated Bradley and Craven Machinery.

At the beginning of 1939 Bradley and Craven exhibited at the British Industries Fair in Birmingham. As a result, enquiries were received from all over the world. Unfortunately, before these could come to fruition the second world war broke. Once again the firm turned over its resources to the manufacture of machinery for war factories, producing some 15000 tons of machinery - a truly grand war effort! On the cessation of hostilities the company began clayworking and sheet metalworking again. However, by 1947 the sheet metal side of the business was sold to Butterley Co Ltd to allow Cravens to concentrate on clayworking machinery.

The 1970s brought difficult trading conditions for the industry with the number of active suppliers of machinery to the clayworking industry dwindling to a mere handful. In order to secure a better position in the market, Bradley and Craven pooled resources with the small Leeds firm of Thos C Fawcett. This business, established in 1860, had long been a friendly rival of Bradley and Craven. A full merger of the two companies came about in 1972 and thus, the Craven Fawcett Group Limited was formed.

There followed a somewhat unsettled period during which the company took various steps to try and safeguard its position in a difficult industrial climate. The Leeds factory was forced to close and all work was transferred to Wakefield in 1982 after a recession and

Above: Modern-day forging.
Top: The Head office at Wakefield in 1964.

an increase in international activities. An association with the well-known West German manufacturer of tunnel kilns, Karl Walter of Hannover, resulted in the formation of Walter-Craven Ceramic Projects Limited in 1985. This jointly-owned company went on to supply turnkey factories for the production of clay bricks and pipes throughout the world. Another international venture, begun in 1991, was the establishment of Walter-Craven Ceramic Projects GmbH, formed in conjunction with Instalat BV of Holland serving the whole of the European market, Eastern Germany and the Middle East. Closer to home, Craven Fawcett acquired an iron foundry in Bradford, and experimented with diversification into other industries. Unfortunately, the firm's already difficult position was compounded by the world recession of the 90s. The iron foundry had to be closed in 1991, and in 1997 the whole company went into receivership.

But, there is a happy ending to the story. Indeed, the two years following the receivership were of paramount importance to the resumption of the Company's history of success. On 12th May, 1997 there was a Management Buy-Out of the Company. The majority of jobs were saved and under the new name, Craven Fawcett (1997) Limited, the Company continued to supply machinery and spare parts to the clay industry. The new Chairman, Peter Deverell-Smith assisted by: Mike Wilson the Managing Director; Vic Clapshaw the Sales and Marketing Director; Richard Draper the Financial Director; and Martin Holroyd the Foundry Director,

began their task of making the Company a viable proposition for the future. They decided to take the high risk, but successful route of acquisition, in order to expand and diversify the business. In October, 1997 the new Company took the groundbreaking step of securing its first acquisition. Highfield Gears of Huddersfield, a repairs and spares business was purchased and renamed, Highfield Transmissions. Its staff and machinery was transferred to the Wakefield site and the first year of business saw the Company achieving a turnover of over £2 million in sales! This overwhelming success led to the Company's second acquisition in October 1998. BJD Processing was purchased, transferred to the Wakefield site and remarkably also managed to turnover £2 million in its first year!

Today, Craven Fawcett (1997) Limited is one of the few companies with full manufacturing facilities on-site, including its own foundry, workshop, assembly and pattern shops, and also has a dedicated team of service engineers on call. So, this Wakefield company which has been in existence for more than half a century and in the brickmaking business for almost as long, is set to continue with its considerable success into the future. Indeed, if William Craven and Richard Bradley were able to see how successful their business has become today, it would no doubt justify them taking another outing to The Clothiers' Arms to celebrate!

Below: *An aerial view of the site.*

Timber specialists with roots in the 1700s

It was in the year 1860 that the ambitious Job Earnshaw made the decision to set up his own firm of Timber Merchants and Saw Millers. Indeed, Job's firm is still going strong to this day, and although the company has experienced much change and development throughout its history, the founders' name continues to live on in the company's title - Job Earnshaw & Bros Ltd, which is currently run by fourth and fifth generation Earnshaws; David, Chris, John, Peter and Daniel.

Perhaps it was inevitable that when Job decided to found his own business he chose to go into the timber trade. The Earnshaw family had been involved in the industry for many years. Indeed, the connection can be traced as far back as 1780 to Job's grandfather, William, when in an article about Kirkburton and its Methodist Associations printed in the Wesleyan Recorder, he is described as a well read man, a church man, and a woodcutter. William went on to marry Nancy, a pronounced Methodist who even occasionally went without supper in order to save a weekly penny for her Bible class money, and the couple had a grand total of six sons and six daughters. It was one of their sons, Benjamin, who with his wife Betty, produced three daughters and five sons, one of whom was Job.

Job was described by a nephew as a short stocky man with a short white beard, bushy silvery hair, and small shrewd quizzical eyes. Like the rest of his family he was musical and enjoyed playing a violin that his father had made, as well as the cello and he could often be seen setting off in his trap with a friend and their instruments to perform at one of the local orchestral concerts. Job married Ellen Poppleton and following in the Earnshaw tradition they had a large family consisting of seven girls and Reuben, the only boy.

Job embarked upon his working life as a Woodsman. However, when a small lot of timber (or 'fall' as it is known in the trade) came up for sale in 1860, the ambitious Job seized his opportunity to go into business. With the help of a loan from Josiah Kaye, a gentleman farmer, Job purchased the fall and Job Earnshaw & Bros Ltd, as it is now known, was established. Initially, Job sold the timber in 'the round'. However, as business increased it was necessary to establish a saw mill in order to convert the unsold trees into useful shapes. As a result, the company's first mill was opened at Midgley

Above left: *Job Earnshaw.* ***Below:*** *The employees in the early 1900s.*

and remarkably, the company remained at this site for 136 years until 1996!

At first, the mill comprised only a joiners shop, a saw pit, and two small sheds. One of the sheds was open fronted, used for sharpening stakes and stack rods, the other was used for riving and hewing spokes out of oak for cartwheels. Initially, there was no power but after a few years Job was able to hire a traction engine and install a circular saw bench. It was also at this time, when the burgeoning business started to flourish, that Job became occupied with running the business from a small office in his house, Thrush Nest, at Stocksmoor in Midgley. Consequently, he employed his younger brothers, Ben and William, to work as Woodsmen, felling the timber and cutting out the underwood. Job owned a wagon and a team of horses and hired another wagon and team to transport the timber. The slow procession of the timber wagons along the road from Bretton became a familiar

site to local youngsters and the names of the horses: Captain; Farmer; Jumper; and Short also became household names locally!

The wood was supplied by the local estates of West Bretton and Cannon Hall and the falls went to the highest bidder at auction. Different woods required different handling and the Woodsmen had to be experts in all areas. Ash had to be taken down before spring, whereas oak could be left until Easter. 'Peelers' would climb the trees, stripping off bark and branches in preparation for their felling. The oak bark was used for leather tanning and the coppice underwood of hazel was used for hedge laying. Elder bushes were used for making skews for butchers and for baling wool and rags, whilst the cut down branches were dressed and stacked into Cords and used for charcoal burning.

By 1880 more power was needed in order to carry out essential developments to the saw mill. Consequently, the traction engine was replaced by the purchase of an upright boiler and a small steam engine, which was used to drive more saws. Later, the power capacity was increased again with the installation of a horizontal engine and boiler made by Bradley and Craven of Wakefield. A brick chimney, a horizontal bench for planking, and a lathe were also installed. This enabled Job's company to produce: spokes; bars for railway wagons; cart and tool shafts; picking sticks for power looms; cart wheels; rollers for the textile trade; and lids, chocks and puncheons for the collieries.

Above left: *Earnshaw's woodyard at the turn of the 20th century.* ***Top:*** *Midgley sawmill in the 1950s.*

Sadly, in 1896, after a period of failing health, Job Earnshaw died aged 60. His brothers William and Ben, and his son Reuben were left to take over the running of the business that he had established and nurtured so successfully. The business continued to thrive, and in 1900, the Foreign Timber Yard of Thos. Smith, in Doncaster Road, Wakefield was purchased for £6000 and William's son, Richard was assigned to manage the business.

For a year, from 1910 to 1911, the business turned part of its premises over to higher purposes. The chapel at Midgley was being replaced and so a wooden building was erected in the wood yard to serve as temporary place of worship! The building was later converted into a joiners shop. The year 1911 also proved to be a landmark year for the company. It was in this year that a Limited Company was established with a capital of £13000.

In 1914, Job Earnshaw & Bros Ltd purchased the 60 acre Lund Wood, near Barnsley. This turned out to be a very successful acquisition and when the land had been cleared it was sold to a Mr Pentelow who proceeded to build a large village on it (Lundwood near Cudworth).

The advent of the first world war brought with it the beginning of a period of devastation for the Earnshaw family. Three Earnshaw men were killed at war, William died in 1915 aged 65, Ben in 1916 aged 68, followed by the death of the founders' son, Reuben, in 1918 aged 46.

In 1923, they were faced with another set back, a fire which gutted the buildings causing £6000 worth of damage. Although the mill was up and running again within three months, this was not the end of the company's problems. During the 1920s the post-war boom ended and disputes intensified over wages in several industries, culminating in the General Strike in 1926. It was not until the 1930s that business began to recover for the Earnshaws. Further deals were struck, woods were worked, land was bought and sold and in 1939, electricity was installed and an electric crane was purchased.

The advent of the second world war brought with it problems of a reduced workforce and increased regulations. Immediately after the war, the 1947 Town and Country Planning Act came into force. This resulted in the Company having to gain a licence to fell timber. However, Job Earnshaw & Bros Ltd used its expertise and years of experience in order to cope with these

Above centre: *Electric crane in operation.*
Top: *The premises in the 1950s.*

challenges and continued to develop an extremely successful business. In 1972 the company purchased a sawmill at Brigg, near Scunthorpe, from Edward C Earnshaw, a distant cousin of the Midgley Earnshaws.

Today, the business is based at the former Denby Grange Colliery where it moved to from the Midgley site in 1996. This site now boasts the area's largest retail centre for fencing and timber garden products as well as a modern softwood sawmill, joinery department and timber treatment plant. The Brigg site also has a retail centre, as well as a sawmill cutting hardwoods. A specialist woodland management service is offered by the company as well as a range of forestry services. Conservation remains a priority for the Earnshaws. For example a new pond is being constructed by the company to protect a newt colony. The area of woodland around the pond was designated as a Site of

Special Scientific Interest and has been protected by the company ever since. The company also values its membership of the United Kingdom Forest Products Association and the Royal Forestry Society.

The tools of the trade have changed somewhat since the establishment of the business in 1860. The days have gone since the company's telephone number was a simple 'Horbury 3' and prices for a 'best cart spoke' were one shilling and two pence. If Job Earnshaw was to pay his business a visit today, he would probably be amazed at the level of progress that has been accomplished since he founded it. However, he would find the continued commitment to quality and technical knowledge within the family run company a reassuring constant, that no doubt will lead Job Earnshaw & Bros Ltd to further success in the future.

Above: *One of the modern fleet.* **Left:** *The Fencing Centre.* **Below:** *Midgley staff, 1996.*

Building a future in the property industry

Woodhead Investments and Development Services Limited, as it is now known, was originally established as an estate agency service in the July of 1965. Without the fortuitous meeting between Susan and her future husband, Melvyn Woodhead however, one of Britain's top 1000 private companies may never have come into existence.

Before their chance encounter, Susan was working for her father in his business which was based in Shipley. Melvyn on the other hand, was devoting his time working hard to impress the estate agency, Hepper and Sons in Leeds, with which he was training. It was in the year 1958 that Melvyn and Susan simultaneously took a short break from their respective jobs and both found themselves in the seaside town of Blackpool. It was in a hotel in Blackpool that the couple first caught sight of each other. This initial glimpse was to be fleeting however, as they were, at the time, passing through the hotel's revolving door! The couple soon met up again and forged a relationship which eventually led to marriage seven years later in the July of 1965.

Within eight short weeks of marrying, the newly weds, Mr and Mrs Woodhead, had set up their own business. In the September of 1965, at the age of 26 and 24 respectively, Melvyn and Susan established an estate agency service which although Limited from the start, was soon to evolve into Woodhead Investments and Development Services Limited. The couple decided upon an estate agency as their choice of business for several reasons. Melvyn was born in Wakefield and had grown up in the town. He had therefore, an in depth knowledge of the town's provisions and this knowledge enabled him to recognise a gap in the market and the need for an estate agency in the town. This recognition, combined with the expertise he had built up whilst training at Hepper and Sons and later working for the

Above left: *Melvyn Woodhead.*
Below: *The original premises dating from the 1960s.*

property company, Evans of Leeds, gave Melvyn a solid background on which to build his new business venture.

The new estate agency was initially located at 69 Westgate End in Wakefield. Melvyn's father, George Woodhead, was a great help to the couple in their new estate agency, especially in the initial stages of its establishment. George had owned several of his own small businesses throughout his working life including, a haulage contractors, a coal merchants and a garage. His experience, inspiration and encouragement proved of vital importance to Melvyn and Susan. Not only did George give the couple £400 to get started but he also gave them his time and indeed, after his retirement, helped out working on a part time basis for the new estate agency.

The estate agency set off to a flying start and became successful in a short period of time. Melvyn and Susan, aided by George, put in a lot of very hard work and

dedication to build up the estate agency. They were soon in the position to be able to hire their first employee. They took on a woman who proved to be a great help to the smooth running of the business. Indeed, she worked part time for the business until 1968 and was paid the weekly wage of £5!

It was not long before the Woodheads hard work paid off and they were selling houses and letting apartments and flats in Wakefield. Melvyn's ambition however, did not stop there. During the time that Melvyn was conducting his estate agency, he came into contact with different companies and people involved in the business. As a result, opportunities started to arise for him to actually buy properties. Melvyn's entrepreneurial spirit took over and he began to seize every positive opportunity that came his way. Indeed, almost immediately, from the very early stages of the running of the company, the property investment and development side of the business took off and was run alongside the estate agency.

The Woodheads started to buy buildings. After purchasing a building, the company would then refurbish and redevelop it, often turning it into apartments which would then be let to various tenants. Although the property investment and development side of the business proved to be more profitable than the original estate agency, the estate agency itself was successful in its own right. Indeed, the whole business prospered so much that only three years after its establishment new premises were needed to cope with the ever increasing accomplishments. It was in 1968 then, that Melvyn and Susan Woodhead moved their

Top: *The premises in 1973.*

flourishing business from 69 Westgate End to the busier area of town. The couple purchased premises at 71 a/b Northgate for the sum of £7500 and transferred the business to these premises.

Being based in the busy town centre brought with it considerable advantages for the company and consequently, the business continued to develop and flourish. The estate agency gained more of a gushing river rather than a steady stream of clients and business was booming! This increase in demand meant that extra help was needed if the estate agency was going to cope with its increasing workload. As a result, more people were taken on and from the year 1973 the number staff employed by the estate agency rose from one to ten!

Over the following nine years the estate agency and the adjacent property and development side of the business continued in its progression to maintain its thriving status. However, 1982 proved to be a ground breaking year for the Woodheads. It was in this year that the business reached a turning point in its history. The estate agency side of the business always managed to sustain its healthy position in the market place and was always successfully competitive despite the existence of at least half a dozen local estate agency firms. It was indeed, perhaps partly due to the success of the estate agency, as well as the increasing success of the property and development side of the business that the Woodheads were forced to make a crucial decision about the future of their company. Running two successful similar sides of the business together began to cause more problems than it was worth, especially in regard to taxation which eventually reached a ridiculous amount. With the realisation that the property and development side of the business was more profitable than the estate agency, Melvyn and Susan decided that they would sell the estate agency and concentrate their efforts on the property and development business.

It was in 1982 then, that the business changed its name to, Woodhead Investments and Development Services Limited. This side of the business was capital intensive and in turn, less labour intensive than the estate agency. Consequently, the workforce was eventually reduced from ten to eight.

Above left: *The firm's St John's North premises.*
Top: *The offices in the early 1980s.*

The landmark decision to sell the estate agency proved to be a success. The company was soon able to start renting out commercial property as well as continuing to let domestic property. Indeed, many shops and other buildings were purchased and redeveloped throughout the following years. The company faced just as much competition from local firms as ever and often found itself having to pay handsomely in order to secure purchases over its competitors! However, secure the purchases it did and went on to experience increasing prosperity and success.

During the 1980s and 1990s the company completed several major developments. As well as investing in

and developing office, retail and residential space, the company also undertook many refurbishments and historical restorations during these years. Indeed, Woodhead Investments and Development Services Limited won Civic Award Prizes for its restoration work on the Regency terrace - Bond Terrace, and the Georgian Terrace - St John's. In the company's 35th year of existence in 1999, it completed Bullring House, a prestigious office development in the heart of Wakefield.

Today, Melvyn Woodhead is affectionately known locally as 'Mr Wakefield' because of all the property his company owns in the town! Melvyn and Susan's sons, Mark and David, are also involved in the industry. David works as a Chartered Surveyor for a local firm. Mark works for his parent's Company as a Director in charge of refurbishment and building, thus continuing Woodhead Services tradition as a family business! Although the number of official members of staff is eight, the company now employs over fifty self employed trades people on a regular basis. The Woodheads are also active members of the community and make contributions to several local charities as well as sponsoring the local St John's Middle School. Perhaps the most significant measure of the company's success, since its establishment in 1965, is its ranking in the top 1000 of Britain's private companies in terms of asset value. Indeed, the Woodheads do not intend rest on their laurels. Already, plans to expand and diversify the portfolio have been made and no doubt the Woodhead entrepreneurial spirit will ensure that the family business continues to flourish in the future.

Left: *Melvyn and Susan Woodhead.*

Over 100 years of brick manufacture in Wakefield

The Kirk family have been making bricks since the middle of the last century with Thomas Kirk (the elder) trading as Kirk and sons. Although this is a story about the Kirks and their connection with brick-making in Normanton, it is perhaps wise to point out that this branch of the family originated from Carlton Hill on the East side of Nottingham.

In the mid 1800s brick-workers were just about at the bottom of the social and financial scale and as work dried up locally, it became necessary to find work farther afield.

Thomas Kirk had married Sarah Wilson and they lived with their young family in Carlton Hill, but with no work and consequently no money, their plight was becoming desperate. What worried Thomas the most was that Sarah was expecting another child.

In the mid 1800s brick workers were at the bottom of the social scale

He had heard of a small village called Normanton which was about sixty miles away to the north. Rumour had it that with the development of the railways and the establishment of an important junction at Normanton other trades would flock into the area. At that time, around 1861, the village which only had 5633 inhabitants looked likely to develop into a boom town. The railways had arrived in 1840 and the first of the collieries followed ten years later.

However, in 1866, Thomas Kirk senior and his brother-in-law Thomas Wilson set out to discover for themselves what the prospects were in Normanton, Yorkshire.

Below: *The founder, Thomas Kirk (with the beard) wit his wife, Sarah , surrounded by the workforce in a picture dating from 1894, a year after the company was founded.*

Initially, bricks were delivered by horse and cart from the stables on Wakefield Road but brick production ceased there in 1998 and the kilns were decommissioned and are due to be demolished during 1999/2000. The bricks are sold nationally and 100,000 are produced each week with the words *Normanton Brick Co.* proudly stamped on them.

The bricks are still produced by the same method but around the 1960s the demand for mass produced wire-cut bricks came to the fore. Pressed bricks are still required and rightly so. They have proved their worth over the years, with most buildings erected this century built using pressed bricks.

Leaving their wives and children behind they travelled up and were offered hospitality at Woodhouse Green, on the outskirts of Normanton and looked for work in a Brickyard on Wakefield Road. Feeling able to provide for them, they sent for their families soon afterwards.

Thirty years later, Thomas (the elder) and his sons, Thomas (who had just returned from Australia) and George, used their life savings to put a down-payment on their own brick-making machinery and in 1893 Normanton Brick Company was born. It has traded under this title ever since.

The Altofts site, featuring modern gas-fired kilns is now in full operation and production runs at four million bricks a year. Thomas Kirk's descendants are still very much in evidence at the old family firm. His great-grandsons, Peter and George are Directors and great-great grandchildren, Christopher, Howard and Christopher's wife, Gillian, all work for the company.

Above left: The interior of the brickworks in the early 1900s. *Top:* Early brick production.

Warburton's - a local success story for more than a century

The story of Warburton's, one of the most respected independent companies in the country, began over a century ago with two brothers, George and Thomas. Thomas Warburton was not a healthy man. One of a family of ten, he was physically frail and unsuited to heavy manual work. He needed an administrative job. His entrepreneurial brother, George - just back from Australia - offered him a post in his thriving cotton waste business in Bolton. Although he took up the job, Thomas harboured a greater ambition and when a small grocery shop became available in Blackburn Road Thomas asked George to back the venture. He agreed, and in 1870 Thomas and his wife Ellen set up shop. For a time business was good, but after a while the grocery trade slumped. Ellen, who was a good cook, came up with a bright idea. "Let's bake some bread and offer it for sale." Thomas had his doubts, no self respecting Lancashire housewife bought bread - she made her own. But it was worth a try, after all they had little choice. The next day Ellen baked four loaves and six flour cakes and put them in the window... and sold out within the hour. The next day she doubled production and again sold out and within two weeks she was baking full time. The baking side of the business soon began to grow and the shop was renamed 'Warburton's the Bakers".

Whilst things were looking up for Thomas, they were less favourable for George. His cotton business suffered from falling cotton prices and he was forced to close. It was time to review the situation. Thomas was expanding but finding the hours difficult although George's son, Henry, who had joined Thomas in the bakery, was showing real flair for the business. The outcome was that George bought the business and the goodwill from Thomas, and decided to develop the baking business with his son, Henry. Henry was to be the real driving force

behind Warburton's for the next fifty year's and under his leadership the business grew substantially. After toiling day and night in the original shop, he sold up in 1898 for £989 and bought the Diamond Jubilee bakery in Blackburn Street. At the turn of the century Henry also took on his first full time employee, brother-in-law Walt Pendlebury. He also stood as a Liberal candidate in the North ward of Bolton and was duly elected councillor with a majority of 15 votes. Over the coming years Warburton's was to become the best equipped in the North, but not content with this, Henry Warburton launched his most ambitious project to date - the plan to build his Master Bakery at Back o' th' Bank in Bolton.

Hardly had construction began when Britain went to war. Most of Henry's workforce was called up, including sons Harry and Billy. Undeterred, Henry rolled up his sleeves and aided by his wife, Rachel and daughter Nellie, production

Above: *Henry and Rachel Warburton with their family.* ***Below:*** *Henry (second right) and Rachel (on the left) during an early publicity campaign.*

continued. In 1915 Rachel Warburton proudly declared the Model Bakery open in front of 500 guests, including the Mayor of Bolton. The end of the war saw Henry's sons return to the business and business move forwards again, although overwork had caused Henry to suffer a stroke in 1918. He was soon at work again, though and in 1920 Henry achieved another ambition when he became a director of his other great passion, Bolton Wanderers Football Club, then heroes of the First Division. The 1930s saw the "Eatmore" loaf launched on the market, with Henry Warburton becoming Mayor of Bolton in 1930. Another great event in the company's history came when George Warburton, inspired by American tastes, dreamt up a new product that was to transform the business, the Malt Loaf. It was an idea that was to sustain Warburton's until the war.

Meanwhile George's brother Billy had made his own impact by developing a retail side, with the first shop opening in 1935 on a new estate in Prestwich. The year after, Henry Warburton died at the age of 71, he was to be missed by both the family and the town. By the mid 1950s the company began to look outside the family for senior personnel, the first time since the appointment of company secretary Jim Aldred in 1936.

Expansion continued throughout the sixties with significant acquisitions, including Imperial Bakeries, the manufacturer of Soreen Malt loaf. Between 1951 and 1965 Warburton's grew apace with bread sales doubling and 38 confectionery shops operating alongside the two bakeries. In 1966 another chapter in the history of the company came to a close with the deaths of Harry and Billy Warburton, who had played a key role in guiding the business through the war years and had seen their sons embark on a successful expansion

campaign. In the late 1960s the family introduced its Blackpool Milk loaf - an instant hit with children and the elderly and still one of the company's best selling lines.

The early 1970s were a period of success with the company seeing continued growth and acquisitions, but by the middle of that decade profit margins were cut to the bone by rising raw materials costs and increased competition. However, Warburton's survived the difficulties by investing in technology and marketing. The 1980s saw the formal establishment of four divisions as well as more acquisitions and expansion into new geographic markets.

Warburton's connections with Yorkshire go back to the early 1970s with the opening of a distribution depot in Leeds followed by the opening of a production unit in Wakefield in 1985. Subsequently distribution depots at Gilberdyke in 1989 and Normanton in 1995 were opened, enabling the distribution of over one million freshly baked products per week to be distributed throughout Yorkshire. The Westgate End bakery in Wakefield produces more than 700,000 loaves per week employing more than 250 people.

Within the last ten years the company has expanded northwards to Scotland and down to the Midlands with a view to becoming nationwide. Today, Warburton's employs over 2000 people and produces over four million bread products a day. Well over a century after Ellen Warburton baked the first Warburton's loaf, Jonathan Warburton, her great, great grandson, can confidently state that "the next 100 years will be even better."

Above and top: *The Eatmore Malt Loaf sold during the 1930s to 1950s.*

Furnishing Wakefield homes for 50 years

Wilsons of Wakefield began life in 1948 from 11a Woolpacks Yard, surprisingly enough to be found in the West Yorkshire City of Wakefield! John Wilson was the founder of the business, after completing his training as an upholsterer at W & T Nettleton in Horbury. With the advent of the second world war John enlisted and bravely went of to war to defend his country and while serving in Egypt met his future wife Dorothy.

After demobilisation he returned to Nettleton's for a brief period ,but being ambitious John decided to start his own business, he began his life of self employment with the help of his wife Dorothy, who worked at home while looking after the Wilson family. The original business activity was advertised as Upholsterers and Coach trimmers. These were post war years when because of shortages and rationing new goods were in short supply, most of the work was repairs to van and car seats and hoods and some domestic furniture. With hard work and long hours John's business was profitable. The burgeoning business experienced a healthy beginning and within two years of its founding John moved across the yard to new purpose built premises at 14a Cheapside which provided the advantages of a workshop with a shop window. It was equipped with its own teasing machine which allowed John to recycle beds which in those days where mainly horsehair or cotton flock. An eight hour service was offered which enabled the customer to have the bed collected, remade and returned ready for bedtime.

In 1954 John acquired an interest in a joinery business at 16 Thompson Yard and combined with the coach fitting skills started fitting out caravans for the domestic market.

Unfortunately interest in the new caravans was low and within a short time production stopped.

In 1955 after years of hard work the business became a Limited Company, taking the name of D.J.Wilson (Wakefield) Ltd after its founders.

Merely a year after this landmark event, the new company was able to purchase Its first Singer electric sewing machine for the princely sum of £93, nearly half the cost of the building it stood in! This investment improved output significantly over the treadle machines. By the end of 1957 the company had opened its first retail shop at 78 Northgate, the first tenant in a brand new shopping development. Disaster struck on the first day of opening when Dorothy's thigh was broken when a roll of linoleum fell over trapping her for some hours, as she was on her own at the time and the development was so new there were few customers.

The company developed into total home furnishing covering all requirements. In the following decade it also expanded into contracting, carrying out work for Beverley's Brewery in the public houses and stage work at most of the then blossoming local working men's clubs, as well as flooring and blinds for companies such as the Spencer wire, British Jeffrey Diamond and the Yorkshire Electricity Board.

John and Dorothy's eldest son Rodney joined the company after leaving school in 1964. A major setback was in store, in October of the same year a fire caused by fireworks completely destroyed 14 Thompson Yard along with its

Above centre: *John Wilson and his family.*
Below: *The present premises in Charlotte Street.*

contents of carpets and furniture. D J Wilson (Wakefield) Ltd was not defeated by the fire. Carpet fitters and Upholsters had to move back into the smaller Cheapside premises while a temporary home was rented at the corner of Rodney's Yard and George Street on the site of the present car park.

By 1967 the company was able to purchase premises at 8 King Street bringing together the workrooms and storage once more with the additional advantage of a large ground floor furniture and carpet showroom. Centralising under one roof allowed the company to start developing again. Sadly, in 1968, the founder of the company, John Wilson, died. However, his legacy remained in the shape of Wilsons. The same year Brian the younger son joined the company from school to help his mother and brother run the company. During the late 70s and early 80s the company underwent several moves within its different departments. In 1975 a furniture shop was opened at 93 Kirkgate, replacing the King Street showrooms.

In 1982 the company left King Street and moved to Charlotte Street, naming the property Wilson House in memory of the founder. A year later, after over 25 years the now fabric shop at 75 Northgate moved next door to 74/76, doubling its size.

In 1984 a decision was made to concentrate on fabrics and curtains bringing the conversion of the Kirkgate shop to curtains, calling it The Curtain Makers. Within a short period The Curtain Makers moved across the road to larger premises at 65/67 Kirkgate. Following the success of the shop the one in Northgate was closed concentrating the company's activities in Kirkgate.

The Wilson ambition was as strong in the younger generation of Wilsons as it was in John. In 1994 Brian Wilson took the ambitious step of buying the curtain manufacturing side of the original business and formed a new company, B Wilson Ltd. The new company focused on providing high quality curtain making services both to the original company and interior designers. Within a few years Brian invited Mrs Gill Harper to join him as the first non-family director of the company. The move marked a new chapter in the history of the business started by John over 50 years ago. A new showroom was opened in Charlotte Street, called Wilson's of Wakefield to perpetuate the name of Wilson for at least the next 50 years.

Above left: *A caravan interior from 1954.*
Top: *John and Rodney Wilson with the first new van.*
Below: *The current premises before restoration.*

Nothing is impossible!

Wakefield is home to the United Kingdom Sports Division of Dunlop Slazenger International Limited. The company as a whole manufactures and sells a range of equipment for use in Golf, Tennis, Squash, Badminton, Cricket, Hockey and Table Tennis and its world-wide head quarters are based at Camberley in Surrey. However, the Wakefield base is specifically responsible for Sales, Marketing, Warehousing, and Distribution, Finance and Administration of the full product range within the United Kingdom. It also takes care of Exports to the Middle East, North Africa and European Countries where the Dunlop Slazenger Group do not have their own Trading Company.

The history of the Dunlop Slazenger Group is an interesting one which can be traced as far back as 1810. The present day company is in fact an amalgam of a number of famous sports businesses. Dunlop came into existence in 1909. Slazenger on the other hand, was founded over 20 years before this, in 1881. Both companies started to develop their burgeoning businesses and both soon became highly successful in their own rights. Gradidge and Ayres, established in the 1870s, and Sykes, established in 1810, were both acquired by Slazenger in the 1930s and 1945 respectively. Indeed,

whilst Slazenger was acquiring other businesses, Dunlop was busy setting up a sports division, the formation of which was accomplished in 1928.

Each of the companies, like many others at the time, experienced difficulties and had to implement changes throughout the war years. The production of luxury items was halted during both world wars. Endeavours were focused on assisting with the war effort. The skilled workforces combined with years of experience and expertise were put to use in order to produce various products including: rifle butts; aircraft wooden wings; and snow shoes!

After the cessation of the second world war business started to pick up once again and the individual companies were able to continue to nurture further success. It was not until 1959 however, that the present day international business, Dunlop Slazenger International Limited, was established. The foundation of the business occurred when, in this year, Dunlop managed to purchase Slazenger. In doing so, a total of four separate sports businesses were finally joined into one international amalgamation.

Above: *Alec Stewart using a V500 Ultimate cricket bat.* ***Below:*** *An aerial view of the Horbury premises.*

and grew it was able to become truly international, setting up units all around the world including: the United States of America; Canada; Japan; South Africa; Australia; New Zealand; the Philippines; Indonesia; Malaysia; and Thailand.

As the business developed so did the range of products and the methods of production. Manufacturing equipment became increasingly computerised and the product range expanded to include: hockey sticks; cricket bats; golf clubs; tennis rackets and all other equipment for the badminton and squash courts; billiards; bowls; cricket balls; all forms of protective equipment; and clothing and footwear.

This amalgamation brought together the different skills gathered by the individual businesses since 1810. Dunlop had built up experience in the tyre and sports industries and in all aspects of rubber technology. Indeed, the first items of sporting equipment to be manufactured from the Birmingham base, were golf and tennis balls. Gradidge and Ayres, and Sykes were always involved in the sports industry but their original skills were based in leather and wood and both companies were based in Yorkshire. Slazenger had the most unusual background of the four, starting life as a tailors and drapers in Manchester before setting up the sports side of the business, initially in Manchester, later moving to London.

Although Dunlop Slazenger International Limited maintained its roots and long held tradition in the Yorkshire area, with factories in Horbury, Barnsley, Normanton and Wakefield, different manufacturing units were also established elsewhere. Other parts of the United Kingdom became bases for the company including; Liverpool; London; Safron Walden; Redditch; and Glasgow. As the company flourished

The year 1996 was an important one in the history of the company. It was in this year that, backed by Venture Capitalist Cin Ven, the company became a private MBO company following its buy out from BTR Plc in the same year. The company went on from strength to strength and today it owns the sporting brands of Dunlop; Slazenger; Maxfli; Carlton and Goudie and has become one of the leading sports equipment companies in the world. Indeed, the company's products are known and used by sporting champions internationally.

The Wakefield branch of the company continues to thrive to this day and in doing so upholds the Dunlop Slazenger Group's long standing connection to the area. Indeed, the UK Sports Division in Wakefield takes a keen interest in the community and amongst other projects, sponsors the Yorkshire Schools Cricket Competition. The company's philosophy is that 'People Make the Difference' and with the help of its employees, the Wakefield division of the company hopes to achieve further success in the future, proving its axiom that, 'Nothing is Impossible'.

Above: *Tim Henman who uses a Slazenger Pro Series racket.* ***Top:*** *The Carr Gate premises.* ***Right:*** *Jack Nicklaus, who uses Maxfli.*

Digging deeper into the national history of coal mining

At one time more men worked in mining than in any other single industry in England. It is partly due to this that coal mining has secured a special place in the nation's memory. Therefore, when in 1988 a new and exciting attraction opened in Wakefield, now known as The National Coal Mining Museum for England, it was bound to be extremely popular. Indeed, originally the museum was known as the Yorkshire Mining Museum but in 1995, due to the success of the project, it achieved national status and was able to open under its current name.

The museum is based at Caphouse Colliery, on the western edge of the Yorkshire coalfield, from which coal has been mined since the eighteenth century. A plan, dated 1971 and showing workings from 1789 to 1795, includes a shaft on the Caphouse site. This makes it one of the oldest shafts still in everyday use in Britain today. The colliery has seen several owners come and go over its long history. During the eighteenth century it was worked by the Milnes family of Flockton but was closed for several years at the beginning of the nineteenth century. In 1827 the Lister Kaye family of Denby Grange took over the work until they fell into financial difficulties in 1917. After 1917 the colliery was owned by a company which included the ex-manager, Percy Greaves and in 1941 it was bought by Arthur Sykes of Lockwood and Elliot who remained the owner until nationalisation in 1947. In 1980 underground roadways between Caphouse Colliery and Denby Grange Colliery were connected and the two collieries merged. By 1986 however, the coal at Caphouse was exhausted and its conversion to a museum began.

The Caphouse Colliery was chosen over Walton Colliery for the site of The National Coal Mining Museum for England, as it is now known, because of its surface buildings, the wooden headgear and the steam winder at No 1 Shaft. The location of Caphouse Colliery was another deciding factor. It is situated in a 17 acre rural setting and is located close to junction 40 of the M1 and junction 29 of the M62, making it easily accessible to the whole of the North of England. The area eventually chosen to house the underground exhibits was the New Hards pit bottom area of No 1 Shaft. The shaft had been deepened to this

*Below: Colliery sinkers in 1913. **Bottom:** Caphouse Colliery in the early 20th century.*

seam in 1876 and was in continuous daily use until 1974. Since 1977 the pit bottom area had deteriorated and it took much work and expense to prepare the shaft and make the pit bottom usable as a museum. This task was accomplished however, and the work that began in February 1986 to convert the colliery to a museum was completed in June 1988.

The museum offers an unusual combination of exciting and enjoyable experiences and by bringing the colliery to life, provides a genuine insight into the hard working lives of miners through the ages. Caphouse Colliery is not what is usually considered a typical colliery as there was no mining village as such because of its situation in a pleasant rural setting. However, the buildings which remain on the site show how a small family pit developed over two centuries. The museum is far from stuffy and the hands-on approach enables the visitor to imagine the scenes of a working pit. The wheels on the headstock would have been turning and the smell of steam and hot oil would have filled the air. The piston rods of the steam-winding engine would have been pumping and the miners walking over to the shaft would not yet be in orange overalls, but in old jackets and trousers thick with coal dust!

The highlight of any visit is the underground tour guided by an experienced local miner but the: genuine pit ponies; train ride; machinery displays; steam winder; pithead baths; nature trail; visitors centre; and cafe and shop provide ample entertainment above ground. The museum is also used for conferences, functions and parties which help to fund the running of the museum. Although the mine is no longer working it is still regulated by the Mines and Quarries Act and has to be run by a qualified mine manager with engineers, deputies, electricians and fitters. The shaft is inspected every day for gas and the mine is ventilated by a fan so that the air is fit to breathe and pumps ensure that the underground workings cannot flood.

This combination of facilities at The National Coal Mining Museum for England enables the visitor to be transported back in time to the reality of life as a miner working at Caphouse Colliery and, in doing so, dig deeper into the unique history of the industry.

Above left: *Denby Grange breaking through to Caphouse in the late 1970s.* ***Top:*** *The working pit site in 1983.* ***Below:*** *The Museum today.*

The Bull Ring from the Cathedral Tower

Acknowledgments

The publishers are grateful to the following individuals and organisations for their help in compiling this book, and for allowing us to reproduce photographs from their collections:

Mr John Booth and Mr Hugh Mayfield of the Newton Bar Planning Department of Wakefield MDC; Mr John Goodchild for his support, enthusiasm and unrivalled local knowledge; Mrs L Ziegler; the unsung heroes of the Wakefield WRVS office; Mrs Kate Taylor at the Civic Society; Mrs Brenda Heywood at the Council Press Office; Geoff Lumb, transport enthusiast of Huddersfield; Richard Hall of Dewsbury Bus Museum; aerial photographs from Wood Visual Communications Ltd, Bradford; Brian Yeadon and his colleagues at the Police photographic department, Wakefield.

Thanks are also due to
Peggy Burns and Kevin McIlroy who penned the editorial text and
Ann Ramsdale for her copywriting skills